Nature of Wollaton Park

Produced by UKGiclee.co.uk
Published in 2021 by ArtCircus Books

ISBN 978-1-913425-21-0

Nature of Wollaton Park

By Oliver Smith

Foreword

Oliver Smith: Author and Photographer.

This book sets out to demonstrate how Wollaton Hall and Park is a key part of our natural heritage, and a leading contributor to natural history education in the Nottingham area and beyond. Nottingham Natural History Museum, housed within the Hall, allows visitors to identify and explore many aspects of the natural world, whilst the surrounding park affords sightings of some of the living creatures that call it home.

Once you have visited the museum and viewed the diverse collections of preserved specimens, you can test your newly-acquired knowledge while walking around the park. Exploring the park you should see the deer and other wildlife that is active by day, although the museum is probably the best place to view examples of some of the park's more shy, nocturnal or otherwise elusive wildlife, such as stoats, foxes and moles. After a visit to the museum, you might be surprised at what wildlife you can identify in the future.

Photo Credit: Jusep Mo

I have always been passionate about wildlife, having spent my early years as a child growing up within a game reserve in Kenya where my father worked, surrounded by lions, elphants, black rhinos and many more of Africa's iconic species.

Returning to live in Cambridgsehire with my family, I Studied Animal Mangement at college and Marine Biology at Hull University, with the aim of embarking on a career involved in wildlife photography. This lead me to undertake a Master's Degree in Biological Photography and Imaging at Nottingham University.

During my first visit to Wollaton Park, I was captivated by the deer roaming in naturalistic surroundings within the grounds. I instantly fell in love with the place and knew from that moment that I would be spending much of my time here, while studying for my Masters.

I found it exciting that the Park and Hall was displaying natural history (with subjects such as bones, fossils and taxidermy) alongside the local wildlife to educate and convey the beauty of Nottinghamshire's rich wildlife and its history.

The History

Wollaton Hall is a spectacular Elizabethan mansion, situated on a hill within Wollaton Park on the outskirts of Nottingham. It was built between 1580 and 1588 by owner Sir Francis Willoughby and Robert Smythson, a renowned and talented master builder of the time. Together, using pattern books from many parts of Europe for inspiration, they conceived what was to become one of England's first ornate and decorated country houses. Robert Smythson came to be regarded as England's first architect, when, towards the end of his career, he was granted the title of "Architector". Sir Francis had made his fortune in the wool trade. He also owned some coal extraction sites. In addition to Wollaton Park, he had extensive land holdings elsewhere in England, including the family's main estate of Middleton, near Tamworth. However, it was in Nottingham where he decided to create, in Wollaton Hall, a monument to his wealth, culture and intellect. He had hoped to attract nobility and royalty to this edifice, and must have been very disappointed that Queen Elizabeth 1 never came to visit. Over the years, however, Wollaton Hall was to be the place that many generations of the Willoughby family would call their own. In 1924/5, it was purchased from the family by the Nottingham Corporation (now Nottingham City Council) as a place to relocate the Corporation's extensive natural history collections. In 1926, Nottingham Natural History Museum opened to the public in its new home. Sir Francis Willoughby's great grandson, also named Francis Willoughby, was a well-known 17th Century naturalist – so it is very appropriate that the Hall should have become home to a much-loved natural history museum.

Sir Francis Willoughby:
Wollaton hall's builder.

Francis Willoughby:
The naturalist.

Francis Willoughby the naturalist was a Cambridge-educated mathematician and natural historian. His love for nature developed while studying under John Ray, a Cambridge University lecturer who later left his position for refusing to take an oath of uniformity. The pair decided to travel Europe for three years, studying the natural world. Once they returned, they embarked upon creating a natural history encyclopaedia, with Willoughby focusing on animals and Ray working on the botanical side. Sadly, before they could complete their work Francis Willoughby died suddenly. In his honour, Ray decided to publish some of Francis's work posthumously. This included the "Ornithologiae Libri Tres", otherwise known as "The Ornithology" – one of the first truly scientific textbooks about birds.

Today, Nottingham Natural History Museum contains over 750,000 specimens from all over the world. These consist of an enormous variety of both biological and geological material. The former includes preserved mammals, birds, reptiles, amphibians, and fish, together with insects, shells, other invertebrates and plants. The latter is comprised of many rocks, minerals and fossils from around the world. The collections are in extensive use for research purposes by scientists and students, as well as for the creation of displays in the public galleries for the museum's many visitors to enjoy. Helping to connect people with the natural world is one of the key aims of the museum. To this end, there is also an Education Room - where children on school trips can learn not only about the specimens in the museum's collections, but also about the wildlife that lives in the surrounding 200 hectare park. The Park is home to herds of red and fallow deer that have roamed freely within the Park's walls since at least the early 19th century.

Many other wildlife also makes a home in the wide variety of habitat types found within the park – from open water to marsh, and from woodland to grassland. Within these, visitors can enjoy watching many different species of wildlife throughout the four seasons. Many of the built structures within the park also contain wildlife - from cave woodlice and other subterranean invertebrates in the passages below the Hall to colonies of bats roosting in the Courtyard roof spaces.

A Grade 1 listed building, the Hall, and the park in which it stands, receive thousands of visitors each year. There is always something happening in Wollaton Park, including regular large-scale outdoor events such as concerts, drama, sporting events and festivals. In 2012, the Hall was used as a major shooting location for "The Dark Knight Rises" - the final film in Christopher Nolan's Dark Knight trilogy. The Hall featured as Wayne Manor - the home of Bruce Wayne, aka Batman.

People visit Wollaton for a variety of reasons: to enjoy the exhibits in the natural history museum, to learn about the Hall and the park's history, to view the deer herds and other wildlife found in the park, to attend the outdoor events, or simply to relax and enjoy themselves on a sunny day – playing ball games or walking the dog. The Hall and park have much to offer people of all ages – from young children to those of mature years. Enriched with amazing wildlife, walks and a fascinating museum, Wollaton Hall and Park is truly a jewel within the otherwise largely urban environment of Nottingham.

GAZELLE
Gazella sp.

IMPALA
Aepyceros melampus

WATERBUCK
Kobus ellipsiprymnus

ROAN ANTELOPE
Hippotragus equinus

**The Duke of
Portland** 1857–
Welbeck Colled

The birds in these dioramas
of a large collection
museum in 1949 by the D
Portland of the Welbeck Esta
Nottinghamshire.

They were collected over ma
during hunting parties by se
the Dukes of Portland, most
William Cavendish-Bentinck
Duke, who died in 1943. The
come from all over the UK a
many are from Caithness.

The birds were later incorpo
these dioramas in the 1940s
by the museum's taxidermi
Len Wilde.

Taxidermy

Nottingham Natural History Museum plays an important role in educating people about the natural world. Walking through the galleries, one can often overhear visitors saying of the taxidermied specimens things like "I never knew they looked like that!" or "Do they really get that big?" These sorts of reactions show that taxidermy can play a particularly significant role in environmental education.

The process of taxidermy has a long history. The word derives from the Greek words 'taxis', meaning preparation or arrangement and 'dermis' which means skin. Some of the earliest known taxidermists date back to ancient Egypt, around 2200 BC. They would use a variety of techniques to preserve a specimen, including the injection of spices and oils. Unlike the taxidermists of today, however, their purpose in preserving specimens was not to exhibit them for artistry or education. Instead, they would bury them in the tomb of pharaohs and other significant figures of the time. Often, the preserved animals would be pets that had belonged to the deceased – so that they could accompany their owners into the afterlife!

Great Cormorant:
Phalacrocorax carbo

Common Sandpiper:
Actitis hypoleucos

Taxidermy first started to become popular in Britain in the Victorian era, mainly as a way for scientists and hobbyists to study animals.

People would also have their pets preserved for sentimental reasons. In addition, a number of Victorian taxidermists specialised in mounting animals in anthropomorphic poses - to look as if they were playing a musical instrument or participating in a sporting activity such as boxing. Sometimes, such specimens would even be dressed in doll's clothes! Early taxidermy mounts were often filled with materials such as sawdust or rags, with little regard for the anatomy of the animal, resulting in a disfigured specimen. Today, taxidermists can purchase fibreglass body models, known as manikins, over which to place their preserved animal skins. Some create their own by winding string and thread around woodwool to create the body shape they want. There are some specimens in the collections at the museum that demonstrate various stages in the taxidermy process.

A Mauritian pink pigeon is one such example – as it still bears the string and pins used to secure the skin onto its manikin in a natural position, until it has set. An endangered species, it is unique to the island of Mauritius in the Indian Ocean. This specimen was donated to the museum by a Mr Peter Summers in 2001.

Mauritian Pink Pigeon:
Nesoenas mayeri

Burbot:
Lota lota

Not only do taxidermied specimens educate visitors about wildlife, they also have a historical importance in illustrating scientific practices and hobbies of the past. Through the study of taxidermy past and present, scientists are able to assess changes in a particular species over time, monitoring aspects such as morphological appearance, size, genetic changes and more. One such study was on a fish currently on display in the museum's ground floor Fish Gallery. This is the burbot, a species of freshwater fish now extinct in Britain. A sample of the specimen's gill tissue, together with one from another specimen in the museum's collections, and a few from institutions elsewhere in the UK, were taken for DNA testing in advance of a potential reintroduction programme of this fish to Britain. This was so that the living burbots elsewhere in the world that were the closest genetically to the extinct UK population could be identified. However, the results showed that the burbot, once found in Britain, had actually been a unique subspecies; distinct from any elsewhere. This important information would have been lost were it not for the art of taxidermy.

There are some very large and iconic taxidermy specimens on display in the museum. George the gorilla is a perfect example. He is housed in the Africa Gallery on the first floor. George is very old, having been purchased by the museum in 1878. Together with many of the other collections, he moved to Nottingham Natural History Museum's new home at Wollaton Hall in 1926 - where he has been a focal point for visitors ever since. Geoffrey the giraffe, also on display in the Africa Gallery, is another iconic specimen – extremely popular with generations of children over the years.

Taxidermy is not the only preservation technique found amongst the museum's specimens; there is also a large entomology collection consisting of a wide variety of pinned insects such as beetles, flies, butterflies and moths from Britain and around the world.

As with taxidermy, collecting insects was another Victorian hobby, valued today for the purposes of education and display. Many examples, such as the stag beetle shown here can be seen in the museum's first floor displays. Stag beetles are found throughout Western Europe, including in southern England, where they are still relatively widespread. The males have outsized mandibles that resemble a deer's antlers. Entomological collections have the same importance as taxidermy, as they are essential for our understanding of the world's biodiversity, and contain specimens invaluable for scientific purposes; especially in the fields of taxonomy, biogeography and ecology. The collections also contains large numbers of shells (gathering them was another Victorian hobby), dried plants, rocks, fossils and minerals.

9

Stag Beetle:
Lucanus cervus

Chalcosoma atlas
♂♀ *Java*

Strategus cloeus ♂
Brazil

Scarabaeus sacchabus
♂ *Java*

Heterogomphus schioei
Brazil

Megalosoma actaeon
♂♀ *Brazil*

Enema pan ♂
Brazil

Dynastes hercules
♂ *Guadaloupe*

Copris istdis ?
♂♀ *Zambesi*

Megalosoma elephas
Venezuela

Ventral surface

Lateral view

Copris hamadryas ♀
Cape of Good Hope

Scarabaeus hector
Java

Copris nemestrinus ?
India

BRITISH EXAMPLES

BRITISH EXAMPLES

Fam.S.SCARABAEIDAE (Chafers).The habi-
lets of the antennae are well combatted,
and are susceptible of separation. The
elytra usually leave the pygidium uncov-
ered. The number of visible ventral segments is usually six,or at the dimensions,
not five as in Lucanidae and Passalidae
About 15,000 species have already been
discovered,and there is a great variety
of form among these. They are divided into
the following sub-families:

Abdominal spiracles placed in a line or
the connecting membrane,and entirely
covered by the wing cases.

Sub-Fam.1.COPRIDES
Abdominal spiracles placed almost in a
line,but only the basal three or the
connecting membrane,the terminal one
usually not covered by the wing cases.

Sub-Fam.2.MELOLONTHIDE
Abdominal spiracles placed on two lines
the basal three on the connecting membrane,the others on the ventral segments.
(If the claws of the tarsal segments).

Sub-Fam.3.RUTELIDES
(If the tarsal claws equal,the front
coxae transverse but little prominent
in the descending axis.

Sub-Fam.4.DYNASTIDES
(If the tarsal claws equal,the front
coxae more prominent,shorter transverse)
Sub-Fam.5.CETONIIDES
Some of the largest as well as the most
beautifully coloured beetles known are included in the various sub-families.Repres-
entatives of all the groups are shown in
the case which includes the Dung and Sca-
rab beetles(Coprides)lauded in the Scri-
lens,the"Cockchafers"Vol.(Melolonthidae),the
great "Hercules"and "Rhinoceros"beetles of
tropical regions(Dynastidae)and the beautiful green "Rose-chafers" (Cetoniidae).

Geotrupes mutator
Europe,including Britain

Copris lunaris ♀
Europe,rare in England

Scarabaeus(Ateuchus) sacer
"SACRED BEETLE" *N.Africa*

Geotrupes sylvaticus
Europe (Britain)

Geotrupes typhoeus
Europe ♂♀ (England)

Geotrupes pyrenaeus
Europe (England)

Aphodius rufipes
(England)

Geotrupes
blackish,brown below

Calofa cacus ♂♀♂
Brazil

Oxysternus compressicollis ♀♂
Brazil

Onthophagus ovatus
(England)

Scarabaeus lysctun
♂ *Rio Grande*

Scarabaeus hector
♀ *Java*

Thyrania agrippina
GREAT OWL MOTH
Upper & underside

Phyllodes andamann
Andaman Is.

Phyllodes cyndhovii

Miniodes ornata
Khasia Hills Assam

Catocala electa Röb
Europe

Catocala fraxini L.
Europe

Dianthoecia conspersa
Europe

Mamestra lindia
Europe

Polia xanthomista
Europe

Dichonia aprilina
Europe

Jaspidea celsia L.
C. Europe

Catocala pellex Cur.

Pseudophia lunaris
Europe

Urania fulgens
Mexico

Urania sloanus
Jamaica

Urania leilus
Brazil

Urania croesus
Upperside

Urania rhipheus
Madagascar
Underside

Fam. 31, NOCTUIDAE.

A very large family of moths, most of them night flying, and of sober colouring, with antennae usually dentate or pecnanate, and in this the rough resemble the much more brilliantly coloured Uraniidae following. All the few species described fall under the single genus Urania. Moreover with nervule 5 double from the middle of the discocellulars as in Fams. 3,4,5,6, and 9 (following). Frenulum rudimentary.

Fam. 30, URANIIDAE.

Light bodied moths with ample wings and thread-like antennae, most of them resemble Geometridae, but a few genera Urania and Chrysiridia are like Swallow-tail butterflies, and have similar habits. The species of Urania, particularly U. rhipheus (or Chrysiridia madagascariensis) are amongst the most elegant and beautiful of all Lepidoptera.

Tawny owl:
Strix aluco

The museum has a huge number of specimens that have been collected or donated over the years – over 750,000 in total. Due to the sheer number, there is not enough room to display all of these at any one time, although specimens in what are termed the reserve collections behind the scenes are regularly on display for scientific research and education. This book aims to pay tribute to both those specimens currently on display and those awaiting their next showing.

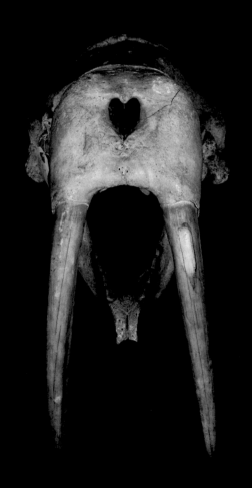

Walrus Skull:
Odobenus rosmarus

Giant Tegu:
Salvator merianae

The Wildlife of the Park

Red Deer

Cervus elaphus

Red deer are one of two species of deer kept at Wollaton Park, and are arguably the most popular with visitors, due to their large antlers and powerful stature. They are a native British mammal, having migrated here from Europe around 11,000 years ago. They are distributed throughout much of Scotland, Exmoor, The Lake District and the New Forest, as well as being found in various deer parks throughout the UK. The fur is reddish-brown, lighter on the rump, and the males grow large antlers, which can have up to 16 branches, known as "points". Red deer are our largest UK deer species. Males, known as stags, are around 2.2 metres in body length, stand about 1.2 metres high at the shoulder, and when full-grown usually weigh up to 250kg. The females, or hinds, are considerably smaller (up to 170kg). The red deer can often be spotted in groups around Wollaton Park, grazing the grasslands, or taking cover under the trees from the sun.

Most of the time throughout the year the stags and hinds remain in separate groups. Mating occurs between September and early November, during a period known as the rutting season or rut. At this time of year, mature stags will compete against one another for a harem of hinds, using their antlers to fight one another for dominance.

You are likely to see the largest stags roaring at one another, to size up rivals and warn them away. If this fails, fights will often follow. Once a dominant male has assembled a harem, he will mate with each of the females when they come into season. After the rut, males and females will separate back into their previous groups. Females normally give birth between late May and June to a single calf. Male calves will stay with their mother for around the two years, after which they will venture off on their own and join a group of other stags. Females, however, tend to stay with their mothers and siblings in a group of hinds.

In the wild, red deer are an important part of our ecosystem – providing a source of carrion to scavengers such as red foxes, pine martens, and common buzzards. In Scotland living calves, too, are occasionally taken by both golden and sea eagles. However, due to an absence in the UK of their main natural predators, grey wolves, red deer numbers in the wild, particularly in Scotland, are much too high. This is preventing the regeneration of native woodland, and thus damaging ecosystems.

Fallow Deer

Dama dama

Smaller than red deer, fallow deer are the other species of deer living in Wollaton Park. During the summer, they have a light brown coat spotted with white – and thus rather more ornamental in appearance than the red deer. In the winter months, however, the coat becomes longer and more grey in colour, dimming the white spots. The males, known as bucks, are the only British deer to have "palmate" antlers, so called because they are considered to resemble the shape of a hand. An adult fallow deer buck is usually around 150cm in length 90cm high at the shoulder, and weighs around 80kg. As with red deer, the females, or does, are considerably smaller.

The history of fallow deer in the UK is strongly linked to deer parks. The first herds were introduced to Britain during the Roman period, and kept in smallish enclosures. Over time they were introduced into larger deer parks. Very popular in the 13th and 14th centuries, interest in deer parks gradually declined and many closed, with the deer escaping and becoming established in the wild. Although a non-native species to the UK, fallow deer are naturalised here, and numbers are increasing. Due to their consumption of crops and browsing of trees, feral fallow deer populations frequently come into conflict with both farmers and foresters.

Their diet consists mainly of grasses, but they also eat herbaceous plants – including brambles, browse broadleaved trees, and feed upon fallen sweet chestnuts, acorns and beech mast in the autumn. As with red deer, the rutting season is between September and early November, and bucks fight for control of a harem of females, known as does. The young, or fawns, are born between June and July the following year, after a long gestation period of 234 days. Young bucks start to develop their antlers at the age of two. Fallow deer occur throughout Wollaton Park and can be seen at any time of day.

Grey Heron

Ardea cinerea

The grey heron can be seen frequently in the park throughout the year, mostly in the vicinity of the lake, where they are often spotted standing near to the water's edge or in the reed bed, looking for food. Identifying a grey heron is quite easy: it is a has a grey back, long legs, a long blade-like yellow bill and a snake-like neck covered in white feathers streaked with black. They can be found near ponds, rivers and marshes, as well as lakes. They are one of the UK's largest resident birds, reaching heights of up to 100cm with a wingspan up to 195cm, and up-close can look quite fierce.

Herons are adept hunters, using their long slender beak to catch their prey. You can often spot them waiting patiently over shallow water with neck arched, ready to strike. They often stand still for long periods of time, waiting for unsuspecting prey to come within striking range. As opportunistic feeders, they have a wide-ranging diet, though they most commonly feed upon fish and crustaceans. Normally solitary hunters, they are known to be defensive over their feeding territory. However, if the feeding area is small relative to the number of herons inhabiting an area, it is possible to see small groups hunting together, as it becomes difficult for individuals to maintain a territory.

Grey herons also become social during the breeding period, when they come together to nest in colonies. A group do so each year in the trees on the small island in Wollaton Park Lake. Their nests are made from sticks, reeds and grasses. The males will fly off to find suitable building material and bring it back for the females to use in nest construction. When nesting, grey herons choose groups of trees that provide shelter and are within close flying distance to food. Females usually lay between 2 and 6 sky-blue eggs, with both parents taking turns to incubate them for 25 days. The newly-hatched young are naked and blind, but after seven days their feathers start to grow. Juvenile herons are a dark grey colour and take around 50 days to fledge.

Wollaton Park is a very favourable habitat for grey herons, as it is so diverse and suitable food is plentiful; especially in and around the lake. Their numbers in the UK generally do tend to suffer during bad winters when ponds and lakes freeze over. However, due to the relatively mild winters in recent years, grey heron numbers have been steadily increasing. This is great news for both the species and the nature lover!

Eurasian Coot

Fulica atra

The Eurasian coot is a well-known waterbird found all over the UK. Coots belong to the family Rallidae, which also contains rails, crakes and moorhens. The largest British member of this family, the Eurasian coot has an entirely jet black plumage, with a white beak and a prominent white horny plate on the forehead, known as the frontal shield. This acts as a defence mechanism while the bird is foraging for food, and as a protection from the beaks of other coots during a fight. Their range is rather broad and in addition to Europe and Asia, they are also found in parts of Africa, and as introductions to New Zealand and Australia.

The park lake is home to a large number of coots, and they can often be seen mixing with other waterfowl as they scavenge for food. They breed between March and July, and during this period, visitors will be able to see them in a different light. The males become very aggressive and territorial towards each other, often fighting ferociously by using their feet and beak as weapons. Once a male has established his dominance and found a suitable mate, they will pair up and build a nest together. The nest is constructed of twigs, leaves, bark and stems, either in shallow water or amongst emergent vegetation.

Females will lay between 6 and 10 eggs and incubate them for around 21 days. Upon hatching, the young are very advanced and able to feed themselves almost immediately, though their parents will feed them too. Hatchlings have red and yellow feathers around their heads and black feathers on the rest of their body. As they mature, the red and yellow feathers start to fade and turn black. Their bill remains rather small for a quite a long time, and the frontal shield is slow to develop.

The Eurasian coot is an omnivorous feeder, with a diet consisting of various aquatic and waterside plants, but also molluscs, worms, shrimps and insects such as beetles. This wide-ranging diet has been a pivotal factor in helping them to adapt to life in different regions around the world.

Canada Goose

Branta canadensis

The Canada goose is the largest species of goose found in Europe. Originally introduced as an ornamental bird from Canada, it has now become widespread throughout the UK. Males and females look very much alike, although males are on average larger and heavier than females. Both sexes have brown feathers finely-streaked with white, and a jet-black head and neck with a white oval patch near the eye.

Sociable and noisy birds, they are most commonly found around the lake, but can also be seen in other areas grazing on grass. Their preferred habitat is around water that has nearby areas of open grassland for them to graze. They are herbivorous and feed mainly upon grass, but also consume other vegetable material such as roots and fruits. They can cause damage to grassland areas, particularly farm pastures, as they are often present in very large numbers. They can also have an adverse effect upon agricultural crops.

In their native North America, Canada geese are migratory, but the populations in the UK, Ireland and Scotland are not, and colonies will reside in the same area indefinitely.

Canada geese mate for life, making twig nests lined with down from their own bodies. These are normally situated near water in a sheltered area, making it harder for predators to find. The male defends his territory aggressively, and continues to do so until the young leave the nest. Goslings are covered in yellowish-olive down upon hatching, and are immediately able to swim off and find food for themselves - although under the close supervision of both parents. After 48 days they will have fledged, but remain with their parents until the following year's breeding season.

Mandarin Duck

Aix galericulata

A more unusual bird that may be seen on Wollaton Park lake is the beautifully coloured Mandarin duck. Native to the China and Japan, it was introduced to the UK, either through escapes from exotic waterfowl collections, or due to deliberate releases. It has now spread widely, and is well-established here. However, it is considered to have little impact upon our native waterbirds. This is partly because it nests in tree holes rather than on the ground or on the water – thereby avoiding competition for breeding sites with the latter. Females will find a natural cavity in a tree, often quite high up, which they line with down and feathers. Between 9 and 12 eggs are normally laid, and then incubated for around thirty days until they hatch. The males play no part in the incubation of the eggs, though they do remain with the female during the incubation period.

Once the young have hatched they have the daunting task of leaving their tree home by jumping to the ground, this normally happens just 24 hours after hatching. The ducklings will then stay with their mother for around forty-five days until fledging - when they will fly off to join a new flock.

The male, or drake, Mandarin duck is normally extremely colourful, with a flamboyant multi-coloured crest resembling a lion's mane. His feathers are a mixture of orange, black and white and his bill is a deep red colour. In contrast, the females are much more sombre, having a light grey plumage with splashes of white and brown. However, after breeding, the drake will moult over a period of time, to eventually be replaced with a plumage closely resembling that of the female; his red beak being the only way to tell them apart. The drakes of many duck species do this – it is known as going into "eclipse" plumage. As autumn approaches, they will moult again, back into their normal colours. Males and female Mandarin ducks often only pair for one season, with new mates being sought in the autumn.

Food is rather varied for the Mandarin duck. They will eat seeds, nuts acorns, aquatic plants, snails and small fish. They normally prefer to feed at dusk or dawn, but around the lake at Wollaton, they won't turn down the opportunity of bird seed offered by visitors!

Eurasian Jay

Garrulus glandarius

A member of the crow family, the Eurasian jay is found from western Europe right across to eastern Asia. It is pinkish brown in colour, with wing patches formed from striking blue-and-black banded feathers. Jays are fairly elusive birds that like to hide in the tree tops and amongst dense foliage, which means that spotting them around the park may be difficult. However, their "screaming" calls often give their location away, followed by a flash of white rump as they fly to another well–hidden spot. Their favourite food is acorns, and they will bury these in the ground to ensure they have a source of food during the winter months. This not only helps the jay to survive, but also helps the oak tree to spread its seeds. Jays will also eat the seeds and berries of other plants, together with invertebrates such as caterpillars and beetles along with the eggs and chicks of smaller birds. Males and females form long-term pairs and are solitary nesters. Both parents will build a deep cup-shaped nest made from twigs, and lined with fine plant material and hair. In this, 4 to 6 eggs are laid, the incubation of which is shared by both parents.

Garden Bumble Bee

Bombus hortorum

Large hairy members of the bee family, bumblebees are often thought of as the friendly giants of the insect world. They are not aggressive, and although they do possess a sting - only use it if provoked, as a last resort. There are 25 bumblebee species in the UK, including one that has been reintroduced (the short-haired bumblebee, *Bombus subterraneus*). The species shown here in Wollaton Park is the garden bumblebee. It is banded yellow and brown, and has an abdomen tipped with pure white. The long fine hairs that clothe the body collect pollen, which the bee periodically combs off into cavities on the rear legs known as pollen baskets. A social insect, the garden bumblebee lives in colonies of up to 200 bees with a single queen. In the spring, after hibernation, the queen emerges and builds an underground nest of moss and dried grass, where she then lays her eggs. These hatch into worker bees, which are sterile females. The worker bee's role in the hive is to collect pollen and nectar, which is then fed to the developing grubs. In late summer, new queens and males are produced. After mating, the queens hibernate and the cycle begins again, with each queen building a nest the following spring.

Amongst our most important pollinators, bumblebees are a vital part of the ecosystem. Sadly, the UK has seen a large decline in the numbers of many bumblebee species. Factors thought to have led to this decline include habitat loss or fragmentation due to intensive farming methods and urban development. Pesticides such as neonicotinoids, which are used to protect crops, can damage the development of the larval bees, and can also affect the brains of the adult bees, causing them to forget where their foraging areas are located.

Marmalade Hoverfly

Episyrphus balteatus

Hoverflies are a fascinating group of insects. Often confused with bees or wasps, they are in fact members of the order Diptera, or fly family. The one shown here, the marmalade hoverfly, is a common species in Wollaton Park. The colouration of this group of flies has evolved to mimic the bright warning colours of bees and wasps. This helps to ensure that potential predators such as insect-eating birds will mistake them for stinging insects and leave them well alone – even though they are harmless! So, if you do see one around the park don't be scared, take a deep breath and look closely, you may be surprised. This may not be so easy if you have a real fear of bees or wasps but there is a simple way to tell the hoverfly from a stinger. Bees and wasps have two pairs wings whereas hoverflies, like all flies have only one pair.

Bibliography

The History & Taxidermy

Anglotopia.net. (2018). Great British Houses: Wollaton Hall – An Elizabethan Palace That May Look Familiar from the Batman Films. [online] Available at: https://www.anglotopia.net/british-history/great-british-houses-wollaton-hall/ [Accessed 2 Aug. 2018].

Cactus on the Blue. (2018). The Importance of Taxidermy Today. [online] Available at: http://www.cactusontheblue.com/forever-young-the-place-of-taxidermy-in-modern-society/ [Accessed 2 Aug. 2018].

Ipfs.io. (2018). Burbot. [online] Available at: https://ipfs.io/ipfs/QmXoypizjW3WknFiJnKLwHCnL72vedxjQkDDP1mXWo6uco/wiki/Burbot.html [Accessed 2 Aug. 2018].

References

Lessard, B., Whiffin, A. and Wild, A. (2017). A Guide to Public Engagement for Entomological Collections and Natural History Museums in the Age of Social Media. Annals of the Entomological Society of America, 110(5), pp.467-479.

Linda Hall Library. (2018). Francis Willughby - Scientist of the Day - Linda Hall Library. [online] Available at: https://www.lindahall.org/francis-willughby/ [Accessed 2 Aug. 2018].

News.bbc.co.uk. (2018). BBC NEWS | England | Nottinghamshire | Experts relocate antique gorilla. [online] Available at: http://news.bbc.co.uk/1/hi/england/nottinghamshire/4357141.stm [Accessed 2 Aug. 2018].

Nhm.ac.uk. (2018). Why is taxidermy still valuable?. [online] Available at: http://www.nhm.ac.uk/discover/why-is-taxidermy-still-valuable.html [Accessed 2 Aug. 2018].

Nottingham.ac.uk. (2018). Biography of Francis Willoughby (1588-1665) - The University of Nottingham. [online] Available at: https://www.nottingham.ac.uk/manuscriptsandspecialcollections/collectionsindepth/family/middleton/

biographies/biographyoffranciswilloughby(1588-1665).aspx [Accessed 2 Aug. 2018].

Nottingham.ac.uk. (2018). Biography of Francis Willughby F.R.S. (1635-1672) - The University of Nottingham. [online] Available at: https://www.nottingham.ac.uk/manuscriptsandspecialcollections/collectionsindepth/family/middleton/biographies/biographyoffranciswillughbyfrs(1635-1672).aspx [Accessed 2 Aug. 2018].

Nottshistory.org.uk. (2018). Nottinghamshire history > Links with old Nottingham (1928): Wollaton Hall. [online] Available at: http://www.nottshistory.org.uk/whatnall1928/wollatonhall.htm [Accessed 2 Aug. 2018].

Nottshistory.org.uk. (2018). Nottinghamshire history > A History of Nottinghamshire: Willoughby on the Wolds (1896). [online] Available at: http://www.nottshistory.org.uk/Brown1896/willoughby.htm [Accessed 2 Aug. 2018].

Wollatonhall.org.uk. (2018). Natural History Museum - Nottingham Heritage. [online] Available at: https://www.wollatonhall.org.uk/explore/natural-history-museum [Accessed 2 Aug. 2018].

Mentalfloss.com. (2018). 11 Things You Probably Didn't Know About Taxidermy. [online] Available at: http://mentalfloss.com/article/13067/11-things-you-probably-didnt-know-about-taxidermy [Accessed 2 Aug. 2018].

Museum of Idaho. (2018). A brief, gross history of taxidermy. [online] Available at: https://www.museumofidaho.org/idaho-ology/a-brief-gross-history-of-taxidermy/ [Accessed 2 Aug. 2018].

Zandi, S. (2018). Taxidermy as an important tool in bird education, awareness and conservation : Birds.com: Online Birds Guide with Facts, Articles, Videos, and Photos. [online] Birds.com. Available at: http://www.birds.com/blog/taxidermy-as-an-important-tool-in-bird-education-awareness-and/ [Accessed 2 Aug. 2018].

Arkive. (2018). Red deer videos, photos and facts - Cervus elaphus | Arkive. [online] Available at: https://www.arkive.org/red-deer/cervus-elaphus/ [Accessed 2 Aug. 2018].

Bbc.co.uk. (2018). BBC - Nottingham Features - Nottinghamshire deer : History. [online] Available at: http://www.bbc.co.uk/nottingham/features/2003/07/deer_ survey_history.shtml [Accessed 2 Aug. 2018].

Education.scottish-venison.info. (2018). Fallow Deer Detailed Information | Scottish Venison Education Portal. [online] Available at: http://education.scottish-venison.info/fallow-deer/fallow-deer-3/ [Accessed 2 Aug. 2018].

Forestry.gov.uk. (2018). Fallow Deer (England). [online] Available at: https://www.forestry.gov.uk/forestry/fallowdeer [Accessed 2 Aug. 2018].

KidsAnimalsFacts.com. (2018). Red Deer Facts for Kids - Red Deer Facts & Information • KidsAnimalsFacts.com. [online] Available at: https://kidsanimalsfacts.com/red-deer-facts-for-kids/ [Accessed 2 Aug. 2018].

Scottish Wildlife Trust. (2018). Red Deer | Scottish Wildlife Trust. [online] Available at: https://scottishwildlifetrust.org.uk/species/red-deer/ [Accessed 2 Aug. 2018].

Tollman, A. (2018). Fallow deer. [online] Bds.org.uk. Available at: https://www.bds.org.uk/index.php/advice-education/species/fallow-deer [Accessed 2 Aug. 2018].

Tollman, A. (2018). Red deer. [online] Bds.org.uk. Available at: https://www.bds.org.uk/index.php/advice-education/species/red-deer [Accessed 2 Aug. 2018].

Woodlandtrust.org.uk. (2018). [online] Available at: https://www.woodlandtrust.org.uk/visiting-woods/trees-woods-and-wildlife/animals/mammals/red-deer/ [Accessed 2 Aug. 2018].

Grey Herons & Eurasian Coot

Heronconservation.org. (2018). Grey Her. [online] Available at: http://www.heronconservation.org/styled-5/styled-29/ [Accessed 2 Aug. 2018].

Livingwithbirds.com. (2018). 21 Facts on Grey Heron - Tweetapedia - Living with Birds. [online] Available at: https://www.livingwithbirds.com/tweetapedia/21-facts-on-grey-heron [Accessed 2 Aug. 2018].

Oiseaux-birds.com. (2018). Common Coot. [online] Available at: http://www.oiseaux-birds.com/card-common-coot.html [Accessed 2 Aug. 2018].

The RSPB. (2018). Grey Heron Bird Facts | Ardea Cinerea - The RSPB. [online] Available at: https://www.rspb.org.uk/birds-and-wildlife/wildlife-guides/bird-a-z/grey-heron/ [Accessed 2 Aug. 2018].

Wildlifetrusts.org. (2018). Grey Heron | The Wildlife Trusts. [online] Available at: https://www.wildlifetrusts.org/wildlife-explorer/birds/herons-egrets-and-spoonbill/grey-heron [Accessed 2 Aug. 2018].

Canada Geese and Mandarin Duck

Bowman, R. (2018). The flawless crowd-pleaser; the Mandarin duck. - Wildlife Articles. [online] Wildlife Articles. Available at: http://wildlifearticles.co.uk/the-flawless-crowd-pleaser-the-mandarin-duck/ [Accessed 2 Aug. 2018].

L.F.Mercer, l. (2018). Canada Goose - of the UK and Ireland. [online] Bird4u. mzzhost.com. Available at: http://bird4u.mzzhost.com/bird_can.html [Accessed 2 Aug. 2018].

Livingwithbirds.com. (2018). 21 Facts on Mandarin Duck - Tweetapedia - Living with Birds. [online] Available at: https://www.livingwithbirds.com/tweetapedia/21-facts-on-mandarin-duck [Accessed 2 Aug. 2018].

New Forest Explorers Guide. (2018). New Forest Wildlife. [online] Available at: http://www.newforestexplorersguide.co.uk/wildlife/birds/mandarin-duck.html [Accessed 2 Aug. 2018].

The RSPB. (2018). Canada Goose Facts | Branta Canadensis - The RSPB. [online] Available at: https://www.rspb.org.uk/birds-and-wildlife/wildlife-guides/bird-a-z/canada-goose [Accessed 2 Aug. 2018].

The RSPB. (2018). Mandarin Duck Facts | Aix Galericulata - The RSPB. [online] Available at: https://www.rspb.org.uk/birds-and-wildlife/wildlife-guides/bird-a-z/mandarin [Accessed 2 Aug. 2018].

Torontozoo.com. (2018). Toronto Zoo | Mandarin duck. [online] Available at: http://www.torontozoo.com/ExploretheZoo/AnimalDetails.asp?pg=584 [Accessed 2 Aug. 2018].

Wildlifetrusts.org. (2018). Mandarin Duck | The Wildlife Trusts. [online] Available at: https://www.wildlifetrusts.org/wildlife-explorer/birds/waterfowl/mandarin-duck [Accessed 2 Aug. 2018].

Arboriculture. (2018). The Eurasian jay and acorns – a symbiosis. [online] Available at: https://arboriculture.wordpress.com/2016/05/04/the-eurasian-jay-and-acorns-a-symbiosis/ [Accessed 2 Aug. 2018].

Bumblebeeconservation.org. (2018). Lifecycle - Bumblebee Conservation Trust. [online] Available at: https://www.bumblebeeconservation.org/lifecycle/ [Accessed 2 Aug. 2018].

Friends of the Earth. (2018). What are the causes of bee decline? | Friends of the Earth. [online] Available at: https://friendsoftheearth.uk/bees/what-are-causes-bee-decline [Accessed 2 Aug. 2018].

Oiseaux-birds.com. (2018). Eurasian Jay. [online] Available at: http://www.oiseaux-birds.com/card-eurasian-jay.html [Accessed 2 Aug. 2018].

Rashed, A. and Sherratt, T. (2006). Mimicry in hoverflies (Diptera: Syrphidae): a field test of the competitive mimicry hypothesis. Behavioral Ecology, 18(2), pp.337-344.

The RSPB. (2018). Hoverflies | What is Batesian Mimicry & Other Hoverfly Facts - The RSPB. [online] Available at: https://www.rspb.org.uk/birds-and-wildlife/wildlife-guides/other-garden-wildlife/insects-and-other-invertebrates/flies/hoverfly [Accessed 2 Aug. 2018].

Trafford, J. (2018). All about the Jay - GardenBird. [online] GardenBird. Available at: http://voice.gardenbird.co.uk/all-about-the-jay/ [Accessed 2 Aug. 2018].

Special Thanks

Dr Sheila Wright, Curator of Biology, Nottingham Natural History Museum:
For supporting this project from the very start and editing the books content.

Mick Whysall, Heritage Assistant, Wollaton Hall:
For sharing his knowledge on Wollaton Hall and editing the history chapter of the book.

Honorable Mentions:

Dr Thomas Hartman, Course Director at The University of Nottingham.

David Mcmahon, Director of Biological Photography & Imaging at The University of Nottingham.

Steven Galloway, Photographic Technician at The University of Nottingham.

Photographic Data

The photographic data for all my images can be found on my website: www.yvesvincentmedia.co.uk/photographicdata using the password: Wollaton

BV - #0077 - 250221 - C98 - 210/210/7 [9] - CB - 9781913425210 - Gloss Lamination